THOUGHTS BEGIN TO

Dance the Merengue

WITHOUT PARTNERS

POETRY BY

Tim Ingram

McKinney Levine Studio, Inc.

www.McKinneyLevineStudio.com/books

*I am the person I am today and
have created the experiences that have
defined my life primarily because of the
influence of my partner Peggy.*

*This collection of poems
is dedicated to all of the people that I have
met and shared a sweet, genuine, authentic
moment including those I've encountered in
my travels, so hopeful that our paths may
one day intersect again.*

CONTENTS

·T·L·INGRAM

INTRODUCTION

It is my honor to say a few words about the wonderful poetry of Tim Ingram. As a keen observer of humankind, a Vietnam Veteran, former police officer (which he felt taught him more about human behavior than six years in graduate school), a trained psychotherapist, good friend and husband to Peggy, Tim's poetry provides insight into the human heart. His words are intelligent and tease our psyche causing us to ponder our own condition.

Tim once said to me that he could talk with anyone. But he was not bragging, it is a true skill. His ability to engage in a conversation with the people he encounters reveals the vastness of his heart and the brilliance of his mind. Not everyone can talk with you and make you feel that they are really listening to what you are saying. Tim can tell a story better than most. His sense of humor and ability to string words together with sly innuendo, reminds me of Samuel Clements. Tim's poetry is like Walt Whitman's and E.E. Cummings' but with a twenty-first century flare.

As a creative spirit myself, I asked Tim about his process. He said that some of his poetry is derived from experience and his imagination. Other poems are inspired by someone saying a phrase or word that ignites a spark in his brain, he will write it down on a cocktail napkin or restaurant receipt, and later, in the sanctuary of his home, compose the poem using simple pencil and paper. After capturing the concept, he will eventually execute the words on the computer, crafting and editing as he goes. The result is this wonderful collection of prose guaranteed to stimulate your own heart and mind. You will be smarter and enlightened after reading this beautiful collection of personal poems.

— Deborah S. McKinney

THOUGHTS BEGIN TO

Dance the Merengue

WITHOUT PARTNERS

POETRY BY

Tim Ingram

SALAD FROM HELL

the implications
so obvious
as to why
relationships continued
to deteriorate
into an emotionally
destructive
chaotic frenzy
when
without hesitation
the relational ingredients
perceived to define
the dynamic mix
enacted by
the parental architects
quite simply
became understood
and boldly
articulated as
a salad from hell

A FOREST OF PINES

within a forest of pines
a solitary lamp
sheds its artificial light
i fear the day
when i might see
within a forest of lights
a solitary pine
shedding
a last trace of nature

WHEN THEY
SMILED OVER
THE FENCE

the animosity lingered
for what seemed
an eternity
like dark approaching
storm clouds
the sadness
and confusion
ended as abruptly
as it began
when they smiled
over the fence

RECOLLECTIONS
FROM THE PAST

footprints echoed
across memories
thousands of miles
from the present

exhumed by experience
not foretold
traveling now
in a timeless dimension

desperately grasping
perhaps
the residue
of the moment

pulling myself forward
cautious
that i havent left
part of myself behind

A HUG FOR YOUR SOUL

embedded within
intellectual precision
a somewhat mindful potpourri
if you will
a thoughtful amalgam
education
experience
insight
awareness
perception
and intuition
at times
feeling a weight
that can best be described
as nearly unimaginable
utter and profound despair
the decline of humanity
like a nuclear tsunami
ricocheting in a synaptic frenzy
grieving the loss
of commonplace civility
and simple
straightforward acceptance
what is happening
remains at the surface
of his thoughts
did the historical
and current meaningful phrase
different is just different
become culturally discarded
in the panoply of broader cultural decay

lacking implications
surrounding what can best be described
as even simple distinctions
of good or bad
right or wrong
truth or falsity
lost in the morass
of pervasive
evasive truth
confusion looms
in nearly every
conceivable direction
frantically searching
for a path
a sign
internally pleading
for direction
even if the comforting respite
is of an ephemeral design
a hug for your soul
is the antidote
which can unquestionably
be captivated
in at least
this prescribed way
embrace
an immediate pivot inward
to bathe
every fiber of your being
in compassion

REFLECTIONS ON
MISSED OPPORTUNITIES

if i could travel
back in time
then perhaps
i may have given you
a second glance
only now too late
the dog days of summer
seem like a century ago
even though i can hear them
tapping at my door
leaves have long since
abandoned their branches
celebrating their annual rites of fall
snow is but a cool memory
creating thoughts of playful mountainsides
the sun is shining now
reflections
that familiar clarity
born in spring
watching the world awaken
finding myself
thinking of the days
when you might have
hugged my heart
now only a quiet reflection
passing with
thoughtful elegance
from an endless parade of
if onlys

A NOONTIME VOYEUR

a noontime voyeur
at a familiar coffee shop
on unsuspecting faces
strangers
im eavesdropping
like a photographer
shooting pictures in public places
on unsuspecting subjects
for awhile only the couple is in view
the children leave
eyes that never meet
darting
fleeting
searching
for what
for whom
for now a relationship of silence
unfamiliar intimacy
married strangers
when did the first word go unspoken
didnt they see the curve in the road
theyre both lost and know it well
neither has asked for a map
i want to scream
stop this masquerade
its too late
the children return
and seemingly make the uncomfortable
comfortable
emotional distance
intimate
coldness
warm
I whisper to myself
do you want to grow old together

A DROWNING AT NEGRIL

at first
i wasnt certain why
the crowd of people
gathered at the shoreline
down the beach
i could see them all
in the distance
thinking that perhaps
the flurry of human activity
must be reminiscent
of carnival times
we continued to saunter
in our lazy tropical way
holding hands
enjoying the liberation
of our island paradise
it will remain
forever too soon
discovering her lifeless body
amid the crowd of people
who sadly had no clue
as to what to do
gently touching her torso
with your foot repeatedly
wont breathe life
back into her body
jabbering ricocheted
like cheesy gossip
among envious backstage actors

no amount of clamoring
could excite miracles here
she died before i breathed into her
she was dead when i left
yet the pleadings continued
when I stopped my attempts
to breathe life back into her
shes dead mon
were my final words
the smell
of the stale salty air
rushing from her lungs
the terrified dilated pupils
of her lifeless eyes
etched forever in my mind
remain my awards
for this performance

A SCI-FI MARRIAGE AND
THE REST OF THAT JAZZ

if you could crawl
inside my head
and see the world
from behind my eyes
i wonder
what you might learn
about living
that i do not
or perhaps cannot see
would we be
oddly
or strangely intertwined
panting disharmoniously
toward the panorama
of our shared vision
or would the amalgam
of our cells
gyrate
in perfect synchrony
from the birth
of our hermaphroditic perspective
and weave a mystical
and more sensitive tapestry

ORBITS

hurled
beyond the stars
by some misunderstood
mystical force

only to plunge
foreseeably
beneath
the flames of hell

troubled
and assured
anxiously
anticipating

the cerebral ebb
and flow
to ignite
another detonation

indicating my
reentry to
that preferred
and habitual orbit

A SUICIDE NOTE

as if meticulously painted
throughout the room
a lifeless work of art
scattered parts of you
hideously decorating
the apartment walls
a pause
a reflection
in your bizarre sort of way
surely an odd reminder
of your last days thoughts
powder burns sprinkled
on the fingers of your right hand
like coarse pepper
on last nights salad
the blank stare
your red life liquid
provides the matte
for this picture
the final penetration
confusion
fade to black
ending dialogue
a succinct suicide note
you win bitch

ON THIN ICE

living
his life
on thin ice
only

a matter of time
before
the foundation cracked
and he fell

into
dark
frozen waters
once again

clueless
where he ended
and
the world began

AFTER MY FIRST
PALM READING

i still
wonder
if
it is

in fact
possible
for a complete
stranger

to glance
at the map
etched
in the palm

of my hand
and tell me
truths
yet unknown

NO EXPLANATION

she built
her life
with
tinker toys

only
to perpetually
wonder
why

she constantly
found herself
sitting
alone

amidst
the rubble
of yet another
sleepless night

ANOTHER WONDERING

if i could
or would allow you
to step over
the rows and rows of barricades

erected under by mothers
and fathers
direction

and touch
the tender place
that i protect
would you cuddle me

softly
in loving arms
like caressing
a newborn infant

or would you
add another entry
to my history
of defeats

and leave me
lying mangled
and wounded
in the streets

wondering
if
im truly
alright

and if
perhaps
i will love again
another day

NO ESCAPE

afraid
of feeling afraid
so he retreated to his bed
thinking that he might avoid
the endless succession
of daytime nightmares
only to find
that his colorful king size sheets
were not an impenetrable shield
protecting him from
experiencing living

AT FIRST GLANCE

it happened
so quickly
quietly
anonymously
an instantaneous lively understanding
when gaze and attraction converge
creating a scented bouquet of passion
that first glance
a spontaneous unpredictable explosion
resonates under the unseen swell of her breasts
and erupts in a frenzy
above and within her mother canal
like the fury of an exquisitely directed symphony
soaring to a feverish pitch
near orgasmic finale
sirens wail
the juice police
fashioned in combat paraphernalia
rush to full alert
preparing to hail
the unyielding enemy
near virgin territory
only one set of footprints
map this territory
trepidation drifts
throughout her mind
like a recklessly driving fog

permeating the oceans shore
seemingly reticent
this reserved exhibition
this unintentional performance
characterized by conspicuous
aloofness
and infrequent glances
preserved the raging hunger
and undivided obsession
that seemed a dubious
and distant promise
still unknown
yet
in reality
lay but moments
from the birth
of its frantic
and devouring expression

AWAKENINGS

ascending
again creating
that subtle
yet purposeful
rhythm
sheltered within
perfect symmetry
gliding on soft light
toward the attainable
lightness

NIGHT AIR CHATTER

a caravan of loaded questions
slick night air chatter
polluting
not welcomed
by a stranger
whose fading mask
no long hides their truth
banal questions
inane comments
deceptively scintillating remarks
of the self kind
an archaeological excavation
to your psyche
uncovers
your shallow charm
desperate wit
hollow intellect
sadly
unknown to you
lost in a complex web
your big bang creation
no compass in hand
the nighttime blues sings wildly
dance on
dance on

BESIDE A POND

(for Peggy on her 33rd birthday)

beside a pond
in an open meadow
tickled by hellos
from dancing blades of grass

soothed by the warmth
of the morning sun
and an easy cool breeze
gliding over the water

caressing my fantasies
captivated
by thoughts of you
and love

NEW YORK
STATE OF MIND

drowning
in an emotional abyss
searching vigilantly
to generate a cognitive map
an intellectual grid
a surge of understanding
an illumination
an avenue of enlightenment
a spiritual flight path
a familiar compass
a meaningful beacon
some celestial sign perhaps
to implant inside my mind
and generate a formula
to assist with a method
so that i might begin
to claw my way
back to the surface
of contentment

BROKEN UMBRELLAS AND
ABANDONED MASKS

the enormity of the juxtaposition
hits like the impact
from a fast moving locomotive
having misjudged the seemingly brief dash
to safely cross the railroad tracks
umbrellas scattered endlessly
throughout the streets of Manhattan
exemplifying the end of another intense
and windy afternoon rain squall
umbrellas exploding inside out
instantly showcasing the now bent and
irreparable frames
abandoned in this fashion
creating a ubiquitous display
of perhaps modern
broken umbrella art
al fresco
pivot intentionally
surgical masks
cloth masks
presenting an array of styles and patterns
inadvertently dislodged from
its rightful user
only to be discovered at some

unknown moment
when the frantic search yields
nothing but
the realization that it has found its
final resting place
at some unknown location
two cultures
two objects
broken abandoned umbrellas
discarded due to the intensity
of a passing storm
lost and abandoned masks
representing not just a culture
but the world with absolute certainty
of overwhelming loss
sadness and grief
sorrow of such magnitude
that somewhat ironically
even within the context of a poem
words to fully captivate
the breadth of loss
will forever remain elusive

CHARISMATIC SEDUCTION

the instantaneous
undeniable
mutual attraction
a glistening transfixed
captivating gaze
rocketing to a shared understanding
an explosive connection
rare
beautiful
electrifying
the reciprocal banter
illuminates the shared
interpersonal artistry
of attraction and seduction
each phrase infused
with a metaphorical nuclear reaction
igniting the anticipation
fortunately
a fleeting
or what can also be characterized
as an ephemeral road sign
becomes quite visible mentally
proceed with caution

NATURE IN ITS
RAW FORM

unquestionably
with precision of purpose
another soul soothing adventure
thoughtfully devoid
of any electronic encounters
expertly maintaining
purity of intent
to experience nature
in its raw form
beauty envelopes the spirit
that kindles the fire
of nearly
indescribable joy
despite its ephemeral
and fleeting impact
the sights
sounds
smells
that characterize this moment
will live within
for all of eternity
the memories may
wain over time
but the emotional impact
will exceed the boundaries of time
like attempts to define
the limits of infinity

DESTINY

i retraced my steps
hoping to find my way
back to your heart
discovering the path
overgrown with weeds
and other unknown things
unable to find
what i had so longed for

DO YOU WANT TO KNOW
MY SECRETS

hiding behind closed doors
drawn window shades
unanswered telephone calls
knocks at the front door
uninvited guests
silence remains
your world is shrinking
life under sheets
the title of this short story
perhaps a wildlife sanctuary
is what youve purchased
a no trespassing sign
erected in your mind
detour
road construction
do you want to know my secrets

MY KINGDOM
FOR A WHORE

my kingdom for a whore
is precisely
what he sadly proclaimed
waking up

embellished in an
unfamiliar
all too common
orange jump suit
in the local county jail

SHE COULD NOT
SAY GOODBYE

she could not say
goodbye
to those
who overstayed

her welcome
so
she continued
to claw her way

back
to the top
of the well
only

to fall back
into
the muddy water
leaving

her struggles
permanently etched
along
both sides

of the shaft
wondering
when she might
climb again

DOWN ON DECATUR

extracting the nectar
inherent in a moment
required absolutely no labor
an evening stroll down decatur
captivated by the circus of characters
embedded within the ambience
of no other city in the world
quite like new orleans
when a beautiful young woman
who could have been
the age of a daughter
unexpectedly hijacks the conversation
without warning
stares intently into the eyes of my partner
seductively and hopefully
says directly
hi beautiful
what are you doing for the rest of your evening
smiles erupt
with fantasies of course
even if ones imaginative ability
puts one foot in the morgue
the stroll continues
silently whispering to myself
words from a film
that will never go out of favor
whatever changing aesthetic sensibilities
may emerge culturally
to characterize and describe
timeless and beautiful art
toto
we are not in kansas anymore

MISFORTUNE

falling branches
escorting murmurs
of a distant wind
plunging heroically
toward a vulnerable
and diplomatic hand
poignantly stirring
with fiery eyes
that conspicuous
perpetual and
elusive grasp
ardently reviving
visions
of shadowy hells

FALLING IN LOVE
(For Peggy)

the beginning
only to be discovered
respectively as that
an erected road sign
in the uninterrupted
ambiguous flow of life
a casual introduction
by a mutual friend
with an almost simultaneous
history unknown to me
of a similar mission
quickly to be aborted by you
preoccupied with the captivating flirtation
of a freshly divorced woman
whose erotic movements
and playfully seductive conversation
seemingly makes this initial introduction
a moot exchange
however, her prior plans preclude
the momentary preoccupation
from progressing into the evening with friends
for dinner
i thought that you had been distracted too
by your earlier in the day
bicycle ride down the beach partner
only for him to discover
that he was not to be welcomed
he had danced his first and last
tango with you
its not as if you had gone unnoticed
eyes the color of caribbean waters
sparkling in the afternoon sun
framed like two works of art

in a color that matched your
red painted lips
golden blonde hair
hiding its invitation to be touched
and twirled the way little girls like to do
radio city music hall legs
breasts that will never play hide and seek
an innocent request to accompany
you to dinner
with mutual friends
and place your ego on display
like a naked manikin in a department store window
will i want to see you again
a roller coaster ride in total darkness
i hand you a piece of me
conversation that matters continues
after dinner and beyond
during champagne walks along the ocean shore
bubble baths too
over coffee fresh fruit and
muffins in the morning
while making love in the afternoon
with fading eyes before falling
asleep at night
after a gentle hug and soft
good morning kiss
throughout endless garden parties
and infrequent noontime meals
(usually breakfast for you)
I know when you became my lover
when did you stop being a stranger
when did you become my friend
a candid camera on romance when you least expect it
that weve fallen in love isn't frightening
that we could fall out of love is like having a loaded
revolver to my head

GONE ON SAFARI

when insight becomes my friend
then i might know a clearer path
avoiding obstacles at all cost
isnt going to win you any
blue ribbons for life
questions remain unasked
answers that cant be grasped
shall you stare at the ground forever
hiding your face behind the web
of youthful hands
trivial proverbs and catchy cliches
if only the rain could wash them away
its a jungle in here
the sign read
closed for business
gone on safari

LYING IN
THE SAND

lying in the sand
yearning
feeling a love
never forgotten
strengthened
with each bead of
perspiration
flying in my mind
higher than the sky
love begins
and ends
with the sun

HARDWARE
MAN

hardware man
coming down
from the mountains
to sell us
your goods

what
do you have
today
to ease
our plumbing pain

I HEARD THEM ANYWAY

i heard them anyway
sobs from behind
the adjoining wall
violating the privacy
of our separate lives

i heard them anyway
late night beatings
disfigured faces
forever anonymous
im much too familiar with your fear

i heard them anyway
objects broken like endless promises
body parts colliding
in a primitive hate dance
i resent the uninvited drama of your lives

i heard them anyway
your double d ranch
despair and desperation
loneliness whispers
softly now

I COULD HAVE TASTED CHAMPAGNE EVERY MOMENT WITH YOU

parting glances
frozen in time
an anonymous street corner
an anonymous city
lacking faith
praying for make believe
outside
the passing frenzy
is a deafening silence
within
a tumultuous tumbling
emotional free for all
damn
the throttle to my intellectual engine
jammed wide open
i once grasped your hand
firmly in mine
we walked along the ocean shore
we talked of love
we dreamt aloud
the stars in the nighttime sky belonged to us
we kissed each one passionately
we wished forevers between us
i could have tasted champagne every moment
with you
we faced each other
hugged like life long friends
respect was our final toast
no pretend to our invincibility
you mentioned love
we cried

i talked of old times
we cried
you didnt need to say
that we were bleeding
emotional puddles
all over the sidewalk
the emotional scalpel
pierced our flesh long ago
as if given direction on stage
we turned in synchrony
lightly touched hands
you left forever
only your memory lingers
in the stale air
im deeply moved
yet stand motionless
the anticipated glance over
your shoulder
as you walk into eternal anonymity
doesnt happen
ive lost you in the crowd
i lost you long ago
its pointless now
to ask the thousand and one whys
instead
i'll be kinder to myself
and bury you
in my private cemetery

I SANG IN THE GARDEN

i sang in the garden
illuminated by the radiant glow
of blossoming flowers
crisp memories of you
also become my audience

i sang in the garden
alone
but not lonely
rejoicing in the unexpected
avalanche of tears

I sang in the garden
louder then softer
frightened then content
knowing lifes illusions
only too well

i sang in the garden
pensive then expressive
sad then happy
accepting no certainties
but death

IF THERE WAS AN ATTRACTION

if there was an attraction
would you hold it
in your hand
like a ball of clay
molding it
in your calculating way
until the pressure gauge
swallowed the red line
or
would you talk
about the weather
and other superficial things
filling the moat
surrounding the fortress
of your soul
flying a banner
in celebration of yet another
impersonal victory

I'M NOT SCRIPTABLE

the questions
seemed endless
an avalanche
of inquiry
an apparent attempt
to penetrate
directly into
the soul
within
the constructed narrative
of my own design
illuminating
so boldly
a pervasive
and commonplace
inquiry
quite simply
understood
to ask
who are you
without hesitation
a most
unexpected
articulation in response

im not scriptable
which
hopefully
or unexpectedly
united
a greater
absolute
frenzy of inquiry
attempting
to answer
once again
the question
who are you

KISSING THE
DARKNESS

leave no stone
unturned
she said
i cant bear the
weight
he replied
kissing the darkness

SECRETS

whispering the night
away
cuddled
in the crook

of
your womb
telling secrets
for your eyes only

LONELINESS IN COUNTLESS WAYS

i thought i knew loneliness in countless ways
the down the street widow whose fantasized intimacy
becomes an electronic trance provided in daily doses
hour after hour after hour
with Hollywood game show hosts
whose spoken words are as far from the truth
as their identity hidden beneath their painted faces
the neighbors little girl
morning after morning after morning
sobbing uncontrollably when her newborn kitten
doesnt come home to be held
and stroked tenderly in her arms
and loved in that innocent way that only a child
and kitten can spawn
an attractive stranger
week after week after week
purchasing a single ticket
in a nearly deserted movie house
dating yet another empty seat
a traveling businessperson
conversation after conversation after conversation
in silent dialogue with their own stream of consciousness
a married couple
meal after meal after meal
as if captured on video
produces their own version of a modern silent film
an abandoned infant
night after night after night
uttering the terror amid the garbage
hidden within her newly adopted mothers womb
another rancid seedy dumpster

proudly displayed at the entrance
to a sleazy inner city alley
sadly a down on his luck unemployed worker
clearly seeking a sort of reprieve from his
desperate and disturbing world
will never truly grasp the significance
of our meeting
completed form in hand
a response to a single question
still ignites utter sadness and understanding
in case of emergency
call no one

LOVE IN CONCRETE
ON URSULINES

another casual
easy stroll
down ursulines
described as such
after all
this is New Orleans
the big easy
destination
the apartment
that is home in the quarter
during visits for years
the beautiful garden
with its melodic fountain
a pleasing
and somewhat
meditative symphony
of cascading drips
interrupted occasionally
by the flapping sound
from the oh so near
roosting pigeons
in search of an oh so near
and quick drink from atop the fountain
however
it was what was observed
during this particular walk
that contributed to a contemplative pause
the words
perfectly etched in a section
of newly poured concrete
i love you

SHOPPING AT THE SPORTING GOODS STORE

the sales clerk
at the sporting goods store
really had no idea
how disappointed i felt
as i left the counter
walking outside
across the parking lot
to get back into my car
after being informed
that he didnt have
my size glove
he couldnt have known
the significance of something
seemingly so mundane
after all
one doesnt typically shop
at sporting goods stores
for their sense of well being
its the simple transactions
though
that sometimes provide
the window to another path
he had no clue
that we werent speaking the
same language
nor living on the same planet
in that instant
he could have conversed
even briefly with me
and sold me something
that could have provided for me
a better grip on reality

SECRET HEROES

at times
there are unquestionably
those
whose acts
of bravery and heroism
in times of absolutely
unexpected
chaos
brutality
confusion
death
despair
and
profound uncertainty
emerge
within this context
to salvage
the lives of strangers
thus
preventing their likely demise
without question

acts that can
clearly be defined
as heroic
and
at moments
initially unknown
to the quietly
clandestine actor
unexpectedly
catapults
to global attention
clearly
not their intention
how many actors
in similar contexts
for that matter
behave in a like manner
only to forever remain
secret heroes

SHE HOLDS MY SOUL
(For Glenn)

a beginning
an introduction
of the interpersonal kind
the dense fog hangs meticulously
permeating every retrospective avenue
traveled down
so thoughtfully
so honestly
toward a recollection of the love kind
the obvious attraction of course
will i see her again
he wondered
cautious optimism bubbles
to the surface of his mind
he longed for at least one more encounter
to captivate an intoxicating glance
into her alluring eyes
to metaphorically and passionately dance
with her seductive smile
and tender embrace
her captivating intellect
and devilish wit
the trap was set
intuitively known to both
consciously devouring the bait
that had been optimistically placed by hands

unknown
the thrill was on
not gone
as so eloquently and elegantly
expressed in lyrics long ago
longing
began to rev the emotional engines
for both
inseparable now
their every thought and movement
intertwined
years and years
have since past
birthing memories too voluminous
to captivate in their entirety
when asked with genuine
and sensitive curiosity
her place in his heart
he replied unhesitatingly
so beautifully
she holds my soul

SURFACE DWELLER

the banal
idle chatter
ad nauseam
perhaps
unaware
of the immense
intellectual caverns
lurking with enormous
depth and breadth
beneath the surface
of obvious mindless expressions
spontaneous engagement
to minimally form
a shred
of shared connection
quickly dissipates
into endless loneliness
sadly
continuing an existence
but
so hopeful
not to forever remain
a surface dweller

THE WOODS ALONG
THE ROAD

(Athens, Georgia)

the woods along the road
an invitation
for morning coffee
afternoon tea
or a moonlight brandy
a natural mystery to be
unraveled
shock waves ripple
throughout my curious side
smiling with intrigue
a dark unexplored
backyard continent
blind to most
a world within a world
i can see you winking at me
one day
i'll stop
and visit you for awhile

THE COSTUME PARTY
(for Sandi)

walking the straight line
speaking the straight talk
leading down
a known
yet undesired
path of mediocrity
leaving that self behind
knowing why boredom and predictability
continuously tug on all sides of her mind
desperate to embrace
the present
a fantasy of her own design
a pot of gold
at the end of this rainbow
perhaps a novel journey
to a permanently desired
oasis of passion
fueled by novel
emotional
intellectual
and sexual explosions
perhaps
at times
merely settling
for a fragmentary and momentary respite
like a two week vacation
in a tropical paradise
an elusive gift of excitement
packaged in childlike form
now you see it
now you dont
too soon though
as reality tantrums in the present

desperately seeking
an illuminated exit sign
a permanent departure from this worn out
groove
recollections
dreams
fantasies
thoughts of
who she used to be
who she thinks she is presently
who she wants to become
how she presumes others understand her
tumbling wildly out of orbit in her mind
tenaciously
tenuously
clinging to the present
immobilized by the past
terrified by thoughts of the future
endless gymnastics on neurological mats
performing at slightly less
than the speed of light
fear throbbing throughout her veins
like white corpuscles
on a search and destroy mission
seeking unwanted intruders
imprisoned
by the child she rears
or the child within
both perhaps
distinctions on distinctions
mind games for you
youve been driving this chariot for years
dont be surprised

if spokes continue to loosen in the wheels
then would it matter
if only you continue to gasp
rather grasp
the reins tightly in your hands
maintaining your illusion of control
your father built into you
a smooth functioning
on off switch
recollections of descriptions
of personal and impersonal history
catapult to the surface
embracing a synaptic plateau
warm tender moments
cold aloof withdrawal
a tribute to George Benson
swallows the night
a departing gift
intellectual dessert
reminiscent of the power
injected into ones soul
like the screaming
dancing preacher
under an old southern
sunday evening revival tent
this masquerade
are you really happy here
in the lonely games you play

THE ENDING DANCE
(for Ben)

initially
the seemingly imperceptible
and subtle movements
blindly unforeseen
microscopic fissures
begin to inundate the foundation
that has united them for years
unaware or afraid
to admit or examine
the slow trickle of
emotional bleeding
evolves over time into
a near steady stream
yet words remain unspoken
now knee deep in paralysis
inaction remains their motto
the ending dance materialized months
if not years ago
known to both
if the depth and temporal aspects of pain
could have only been perceived by either
that it is preferable to experience
more intense pain for a shorter duration
than less pain for a much longer duration
then perhaps inaction may have been buried
with the ending dance taking its final steps
toward that so longed for freedom

THE WONDERFULNESS
OF ME

perhaps
initially
an attraction
to her interpersonal style
often characterized by others
as artistry
initially misperceived
thus elusive
however
pivot to an often used
road map to success
persistence is the plan
still
this did not allow
for an unfolding
of a sweet and/or
mystical epiphany
although the words
continued back and forth
like children
on a playground teeter totter
but alas
the moment passed
and the parting words filled the air
with sadness
and disappointment
I so wish
that you could have seen
the wonderfulness of me

THOUGHTS BEGIN TO DANCE THE MERENGUE WITHOUT PARTNERS

jelly beans
vibrant things
picasso paintings framed in view
balloons soaring from the grasp of a forgiving hand
crayolas scattered around a smiling child
the west texas sky kissing me at sunset
the north georgia mountains dancing her elegance in
the fall
laughter hugs me like a loving friend
fear becomes an uninvited guest
and stays for the main entree and beyond
goddamn it
youre no longer welcome here
lately sadness is my constant companion
entertain my only request of you
place your hand in mine and hold it gently
you hold me captive but not imprisoned
im singing your lyrics
and dancing to your symphony
smile
the music is about to change tempo
ive choreographed new steps
free floating indecision
icebergs colliding in my mind
palm trees swaying on unchartered islands
confusion
elation
one two
lifes tango
tickle me softly now
whisper to me with your eyes
speak to me without words
caress me with a gaze unlike any other
ive invited you

place your heart in the upright position
buckle up your emotions
place your fear in the overhead compartment
your sexuality wont fit under the seat in front of you
suddenly retreat to a carnival unseen
dressed in striped baggy pants
your oversized shoes hide your toes true intentions
red red lips would make a saturday night drag queen
envious
change the channel
turn the synaptic knob
ive changed maps
my heart leapt across the continent
ny to la in my chest
whos driving this machine
overdrive through a fellini film titled living
rest stop ahead
say no to drugs
flight fright and fight
packaged neatly with an off season bow
dont stop paddling this canoe
rapids seductively smile hello
into the night
my life vest unseen
no safety nets here
hand me a balancing pole
and i'll walk a tightrope to your soul
if i fall
my parachute was untied from my navel at birth
when my mother connection was undone
there are no white flags here
the developing ocean is like a dry lake bed
besides
im way too big to crawl back to safety
an unknown waitress served you
bacon and my ego for breakfast

thank you for the leftovers
i'll lick whats left of myself from your plate
vulnerability isnt served by a short order chef
intimacy cant be bought
in a ten minute fifty dollar parade
with a teenage hooker looking for fucking meaning
nor in a downtown xxxx cum house
with rambo toys for the black leather brave
nor from twenty-five cent videos
for those lost in a limp dick median separating an
unknown sexual highway
respite
click your heels
leave this unknown intersection
on a deserted beach
at an imagined island
where the caribbean sun warms a welcomed sanctuary
to hide from the present
ghosts are tickling me now
reality is screaming for attention
like a bratty two year old whos lost his favorite toy
the floodgates are primed without spoken words
beware downstream
you might get washed away by memories
with bleeding wounds
static ripples through a thousand thoughts
walk with me to the canyons edge
im lying
youre already flirting with a fatal kiss
a gentle breeze suddenly whispers in my ear playing
a game r d laing style
playing a game at not playing a game
existential nightmares are loaded into the empty
chambers of my spiritual revolver
encounter with a stranger hits the accelerator
no names please

it didnt begin with hello
i'll leave without good bye
its more exciting that way
for whom
commitments and expectations were removed
as we undressed
tossing them on the floor with our clothes
our sanity lost forever between us
perhaps our pride stays hidden in our underwear
watching blindly this center stage attraction
detour ahead
theres no round trip ticket for this travel
traveling on a winding mountain road
the signs slap my face to attention
beware
dangerous curve ahead
abort isnt in my vocabulary
whos strapped me in on this intergalactic journey
through newly discovered universes
with no language to describe
what the fuck is happening to me
psychobabble bubbles to the surface
regression in service to your ego or mine
insecurity greets me
like the morning sun peeking over the horizon
thank you james kavanaugh
my fear erupts as anger too
a little bit softer now
alone
hidden from view
by ferns the size of cadillacs
sabertooth tigers
and the movement of strangers
with freshly painted faces
leap toward me like characters in a 3d movie
six foot ants with feelers the size of telephone poles

crawl near
a euphoric
no dysphoric
drug like induced
surrealistic
this cant be happening to me
semi conscious fog
is my present state of mind
shit
a brazilian rain forest is french kissing my imagination
i dont mind surrendering to your snake oil charm
i will stay and play in this fantasy forest of feast famine
and friends for awhile
if i have a mind too
mysterious
no delirious
perhaps furious
i didnt receive an invitation
to a south american mountain
chewing on coca leaf
no coffee beans
but plenty of bananas though party
i will drink champagne under the melodramatic shade
until our symbiotic bubbles burst
born from neurological wombs singing the blues
that would make the town cast in a fellini film
look like a group of cpas on parade
im intrigued by the sweetness of your tropical music
thoughts begin to dance the merengue without partners
guava dreams tonight my dear
exit stage right from this cerebral autoerotic journey
the final act is faintly heard
like the sighs of freshly falling snow

COLOR AND DIVERSITY

endless shades of grey
seem to perpetually
cloud his perception
poignantly aware
that the overwhelming
beauty in the world
ignites the imagination
when best perceived
by captivating
natures vibrant
color and diversity

WAY MO BETTER

creating
another personal mission
leading to a precipice
a balancing act
if you will
that continues
its ebb and flow
misery
heartbreak
discouragement
discontentment
sadness
felt
like the impact
of an emotional hurricane
now teetering
push pause
the normalcy of it all
ignites this understanding
avoidance
clearly a failed strategy
pull in the reins
sweetness
kindness
compassion
joy
love
hold on tight
why
the emotional impact
of this tsunami
way mo better

THOUGHTS TRAPPED IN DARK AIR

exploring
in a graveyard of memories
buried long ago
an intellectual reincarnation
thoughts possessing souls of their own
a kind of mind heaven
or hell
mental purgatory perhaps
thoughts trapped in dark air
images with pleading eyes
meandering through yesterdays attic
my emotional kaleidoscope twists and
turns
displaying ever changing designs from
living
a meandering avalanche of experiential
non sequiturs
feeding a widening river of
consciousness
eyes open
saying hello like a red neon sign
pulsating through an open window
in a big city hotel

racing thundering pounding
a team of wild horses
gallops across my chest
eyes closed
like the awkward departure of a life
long friend
stillness
calm air
free floating in my mind
in the quietness
of a slow moving cloud
stepping dramatically
on stones
across the waters of my spiritual pond
retreating
resting yet again
in my sacred burial ground

TIPSY BUT NOT MESSY

unaware of a single clue
no premonition
or hunch
or intuitive feel
not even a slight inkling
like so many others
whose unconscious mind
unknowingly
unexpectedly
bursts forth
like an underground sewer worker
catapulted to the surface
clinging to a manhole cover
to escape the unforeseen torrent of
human waste
clearly
the unconscious mind
generates more than just intellectual
refuse
meaningless and meaningful
understandings
secretly intertwined
reminiscent of the genetic connection
of siamese twins
catapult to a verbal expression
revealing more than just the words
spoken

tipsy but not messy
he uttered stoically
staggering sideways
like the only too predictable
movements
of a down on his luck
living on the streets
brandy in a brown paper bag
drunk
in reality
tipsy but not messy
became his mantra
for living
as he managed to stroll
without losing his foothold
recklessly
clumsily
teetering on the edge
of living his life

I GOTTA GET SOME
FISH FROM HER

at one of the most unexpected
and perhaps unusual places
to potentially find love
while merely on a mission
to purchase a fresh
catch of the day
for tonights dinner
when in that instant
their eyes converged
the menu changed
and he said to himself
i gotta get some fish from her

YOU'RE KILLING
MY VIBE

yet another
in a seemingly endless
succession
of thoughtless
and ignorant expressions
invading
the tranquility
and contentment
of this precise moment
irrespective of content
demanding
yet again
ad nauseam
a somewhat
benevolent response
within a nearly
endless list
of possibilities
to avoid
being emotionally hijacked
into an unwelcomed
emotional abyss
artfully poised
to succinctly
and graciously utter
once again
youre killing my vibe

WAY OUT THERE
(for Steve)

i find
myself
falling off
the face

of the earth
wondering
now if i ever

really knew
or
could possibly
find

of my own design
that fragrant groove
of
contentment

HE'S GOT THE DEVIL
ON HIS SHOULDERS

sweetness of expression
flagrantly in retreat
for some time now
hushed whispers
among those who share
familiarity with his life
significantly more questions
than meaningful understandings
as to why
such an abrupt retreat
to an apparent
but hopefully temporary
loss of civility
this unexpected shift
best characterized
with one particular utterance
among his friends
he's got the devil on his shoulders

WAY BACK HOUSE

appearing
with known
and predictable timing
like an actor
on stage
making their mark
without fail
presenting
with an unrelenting
oddity
in dress
and interpersonal style
known to all
in both
open
and hushed
conversation
rarely
if ever
referred to by name
other than
most commonly
as the guy
who lives
on the outskirts of town
in the way back house
wandering
in plain sight
wondering perhaps
what generates
the occasional stares

and missed opportunities
from others
to engage with genuineness
thus
possibly creating a more meaningful
moment of understanding
however
others blinded by the
oh so frequent facile observation
again hindering
even a glimpse
into the depth
of his loving spirit

RED ROCK
(for Martin)

secluded in paradise
the enchanting view
a welcomed hug
back in time
involuntarily propelled
by a rustic time machine
made of wood
to a slightly distant past
guided by strangers
whose spirits resonate
in playful harmony
trapper creek
now runs
through my veins
in infinite supply

IMPULSIVE

another
rash decision
seeking
intellectual salve
to soothe
the chaos
of his
impetuous ways
he thought

I NEVER HAD
GRANDIOSE DREAMS

once again
in an apparent succession
of methodically
pushing the pause button
not for a brief
or fleeting respite
but for a prolonged
quiet introspection
at times purposeful
other moments
appear random
reflecting with intellectual precision
the life that has been choreographed
and continues to be lived with gratitude
I never had grandiose dreams
became his trademark
embroidered beautifully
on his lifes banner
displayed prominently
for all to witness

www.ingramcontent.com/pod-product-compliance
Lightning Source LLC
Chambersburg PA
CBHW051328120626
46547CB00015B/2445